GUIDE TO POKEMON TYPES

Each Pokemon has one or two types, and types determine much about how that Pokemon battles. For the Pokemon Trainer, type is important because certain types are strong against others, meaning you can deal or take additional damage, or on the other hand lessen the amount of damage received.

There's 18 different types, and each type is either strong, weak or neutral versus other types. At the most basic level with the starter Pokemon this breaks down to Rock, Paper, Scissors – Charmander (Fire) beats Bulbasaur (Grass) who beats Squirtle (Water) which comes full circle by beating Fire. That all makes sense and is nice and easy – though things get more complicated when you start introducing more obtuse Pokemon Types types like Fairy or Dragon, or when you consider Pokemon with multiple types.

TYPE: DARK

The only thing unlucky about Absol is its appearance. It protects fields and warns people of disaster, so one ought to be grateful for it.

How to Say It: Ab-sol
Imperial Height: 3' 11"
Imperial Weight: 103.6 lbs
Metric Height: 1.2 m
Metric Weight: 47.0 kg

Possible Moves: Feint, Future Sight, Leer, Perish Song, Quick Attack, Scratch, Leer, Quick Attack, Pursuit, Taunt, Bite, Double Team, Slash, Swords Dance

Kalos
(Central)
Kanto

ABSOL
Disaster Pokémon

BASE STATS

Stat	Value		Min	Max
HP	65		240	334
Attack	130		238	394
Defense	60		112	240
Sp. Atk	75		139	273
Sp. Def	60		112	240
Speed	75		139	273
Total	465		Min	Max

TYPE: ELECTRIC

The light from its tail can be seen from space. This is why you can always tell exactly where it is, which is why it usually keeps the light off.

How to Say It: Am-pa-ros
Imperial Height: 4' 07"
Imperial Weight: 135.6 lbs
Metric Height: 1.4 m
Metric Weight: 61.5 kg

Possible Moves: Dragon Pulse, Fire Punch, Growl, Ion Deluge, Magnetic Flux, Tackle, Thunder Punch, Thunder Shock, Thunder Wave, Zap Cannon, Cotton Spore

Kalos (Central)
Kanto

AMPHAROS
Light Pokémon

BASE STATS

HP	90		290	384
Attack	75		139	273
Defense	85		157	295
Sp. Atk	115		211	361
Sp. Def	90		166	306
Speed	55		103	229
Total	510		Min	Max

TYPE: FIRE

Legends tell of its fighting alongside a general and conquering a whole country.

Kalos (Central)
Kanto

ARCANINE
Legendary Pokémon

How to Say It: Ar-ka-nin
Imperial Height: 6' 03"
Imperial Weight: 341.7 lbs
Metric Height: 1.9 m
Metric Weight: 155.0 kg

Possible Moves: Agility, Bite, Burn Up, Crunch, Ember, Extreme Speed, Fire Fang, Flame Wheel, Flamethrower, Flare Blitz, Helping Hand, Howl, Leer, Play Rough

BASE STATS

Stat	Value		Min	Max
HP	90		290	384
Attack	110		202	350
Defense	80		148	284
Sp. Atk	100		184	328
Sp. Def	80		148	284
Speed	95		175	317
Total	555			

TYPE: NORMAL

According to the legends of Sinnoh, this Pokémon emerged from an egg and shaped all there is in this world.

How to Say It: Ar-kius
Imperial Height: 10' 06"
Imperial Weight: 705.5 lbs
Metric Height: 3.2 m
Metric Weight: 320.0 kg

Possible Moves: Comic Power, Natural Gift, Punishment, Seismic Toss, Gravity, Earth Power, Hyper Voice, Extreme Speed, Refresh, Future Sight, Recover, Hyper Beam

Kalos *(Central)*
Kanto

ARCEUS
Alpha Pokémon

MYTHICAL POKEMON

BASE STATS

Stat	Base		Min	Max
HP	120		350	444
Attack	120		220	372
Defense	120		220	372
Sp. Atk	120		220	372
Sp. Def	120		220	372
Speed	120		220	372
Total	720			

ARTICUNO
Freeze Pokémon

Kalos
(Central)
Kanto

LEGENDARY POKEMON

TYPE: ICE- FLYING

Articuno is a legendary bird Pokémon that can control ice. The flapping of its wings chills the air. As a result, it is said that when this Pokémon flies, snow will fall.

How to Say It: ART-tick-COO-no
Imperial Height: 5' 07"
Imperial Weight: 122.1 lbs
Metric Height: 1.7m
Metric Weight: 55.4kg

Possible Moves: Gust, Ice Shard, Mist, Leer, Mirror Coat, Ice Beam, Agility, Reflect, Roost, Blizzard, Sky Attack

BASE STATS

HP	90		290	384
Attack	85		157	295
Defense	100		184	328
Sp. Atk	95		175	317
Sp. Def	125		229	383
Speed	85		157	295
Total	580		Min	Max

TYPE: PSYCHIC

Known as "The Being of Willpower." It sleeps at the bottom of a lake to keep the world in balance.

How to Say It: La-Tios
Imperial Height: 1' 00"
Imperial Weight: 0.7 lbs
Metric Height: 0.3 m
Metric Weight: 0.3 kg

Possible Moves: Confusion, Last Resort, Natural Gift, Rest, Imprison, Detect, Swift, Uproar, Future Sight

Kalos (Central)
Kanto

AZELF
Willpower Pokémon

LEGENDARY POKEMON

BASE STATS

Stat	Value		Min	Max
HP	75		260	354
Attack	125		229	383
Defense	70		130	262
Sp. Atk	125		229	383
Sp. Def	70		130	262
Speed	115		211	361
Total	580			

BLACEPHALON

Fireworks Pokemon

Kalos (Central)
Kanto

LEGENDARY POKEMON

TYPE: FIRE-GHOST

It slithers toward people. Then, without warning, it triggers the explosion of its own head. It's apparently one kind of Ultra Beast.

How to Say It: Blei-se-pa-lon
Imperial Height: 5' 11"
Imperial Weight: 28.7 lbs
Metric Height: 1.8m
Metric Weight: 13 kg

Possible Moves: Astonish, Ember, Magic Coat, Stored Power, Flame Burst, Night Shade, Light Screen, Calm Mind, Fire Blast, Shadow Ball

BASE STATS

Stat	Value	Min	Max
HP	53	216	310
Attack	127	233	388
Defense	53	99	225
Sp. Atk	151	276	441
Sp. Def	79	146	282
Speed	107	197	344
Total	570		

TYPE: WATER

Blastoise has water spouts that protrude from its shell. The water spouts are very accurate. They can shoot bullets of water with enough accuracy to strike empty cans from a distance of over 160 feet.

How to Say It: BLAS-TOYS
Imperial Height: 5' 03"
Imperial Weight: 188.5 lbs
Metric Height: 1.6 m
Metric Weight: 85.5 kg

Possible Moves: Flash Cannon, Tackle, Tail Whip, Water Gun, Withdraw, Rapid Spin, Bite, Water Pulse, Protect, Rain Dance

Kalos (Central)
Kanto

BLASTOISE
Shellfish Pokémon

BASE STATS

			Min	Max
HP	79		268	362
Attack	83		153	291
Defense	100		184	328
Sp. Atk	85		157	295
Sp. Def	105		193	339
Speed	78		144	280
Total	530			

TYPE: FIRE-FIGHTING

In battle, Blaziken blows out intense flames from its wrists and attacks foes courageously. The stronger the foe, the more intensely this Pokémon's wrists burn.

How to Say It: Bla-si-ken
Imperial Height: 6' 03"
Imperial Weight: 114.6 lbs
Metric Height: 1.9 m
Metric Weight: 52.0 kg

Possible Moves: Blaze Kick, Double Kick, Ember, Fire Punch, Flare Blitz, Growl, High Jump Kick, Sand Attack, Scratch, Ember, Bulk Up, Focus Energy

Kalos
(Central)
Kanto

BLAZIKEN
Blaze Pokémon

BASE STATS

		Min	Max
HP	80	270	364
Attack	120	220	372
Defense	70	130	262
Sp. Atk	110	202	350
Sp. Def	70	130	262
Speed	80	148	284
Total	530		

BULBASAUR

Seed Pokémon

Kalos
(Central)
Kanto

TYPE: GRASS-POISON

Bulbasaur can be seen napping in bright sunlight. There is a seed on its back. By soaking up the sun's rays, the seed grows progressively larger.

How to Say It: Bal-ba-sor
Imperial Height: 2' 04"
Imperial Weight: 6.9 lbs
Metric Height: 0.7 m
Metric Weight: 6.9 kg

Possible Moves: Growl, Tackle, Vine Whip, Growth, Leech Seed, Razor Leaf, Poison Powder, Sleep Powder, Seed Bomb, Take Down, Sweet Scent, Synthesis

BASE STATS

		Min	Max
HP	45	200	294
Attack	49	92	216
Defense	49	92	216
Sp. Atk	65	121	251
Sp. Def	65	121	251
Speed	45	85	207
Total	318		

TYPE: BUG-FIGHT

Although it's alien to this world and a danger here, it's apparently a common organism in the world where it normally lives.

How to Say It: Buz-Wol
Imperial Height: 7' 10"
Imperial Weight: 735.5 lbs
Metric Height: 2.4m
Metric Weight: 333.6kg

Possible Moves: Fell Stinger, Focus Energy, Harden, Ice Punch, Power-Up Punch, Reversal, Thunder Punch, Comet Punch

Kalos *(Central)*
Kanto

BUZZWOLE
Swollen Pokémon

LEGENDARY POKEMON

BASE STATS

HP	107		324	418
Attack	139		254	414
Defense	139		254	414
Sp. Atk	53		99	225
Sp. Def	53		99	225
Speed	79		146	282
Total	570		Min	Max

TYPE: PSYCHIC-GRASS

This Pokémon came from the future by crossing over time. It is thought that so long as Celebi appears, a bright and shining future awaits us.

How to Say It: CE-le-bi
Imperial Height: 2' 00"
Imperial Weight: 11.0lbs
Metric Height: 0.6m
Metric Weight: 5kg

Possible Moves: Confusion, Heal Bell, Magical Leaf, Baton Pass, Ancient Power, Life Dew, Leech Seed, Recover, Future Sight, Healing Wish, Leaf Storm

Kalos (Central)
Kanto

CELEBI
Time Travel Pokémon

MYTHICAL POKEMON

BASE STATS

Stat	Value		Min	Max
HP	100		310	404
Attack	100		184	328
Defense	100		184	328
Sp. Atk	100		184	328
Sp. Def	100		184	328
Speed	100		184	328
Total	600			

CELESTEELA
Launch Pokemon

Kalos (Central)
Kanto

LEGENDARY POKEMON

TYPE: STEEL

One of the dangerous UBs, high energy readings can be detected coming from both of its huge arms.

How to Say It: Se-le-sti-la
Imperial Height: 30' 02"
Imperial Weight: 2204.4 lbs
Metric Height: 9.2 m
Metric Weight: 999.9 kg

Possible Moves: Absorb, Air Slash, Harden, Ingrain, Tackle, Wide Guard, Smack Down, Mega Drain, Leech Seed, Metal Sound, Iron Head, Giga Drain

BASE STATS

			Min	Max
HP	97		304	398
Attack	101		186	331
Defense	103		189	335
Sp. Atk	107		197	344
Sp. Def	101		186	331
Speed	61		114	243
Total	570			

CHARIZARD
Flame Pokémon

Kalos (Central)
Kanto

TYPE: FIRE

Charizard flies around the sky in search of powerful opponents. It breathes fire of such great heat that it melts anything. However, it never turns its fiery breath on any opponent weaker than itself.

How to Say It: Ar-ka-nin
Imperial Height: 6' 03"
Imperial Weight: 341.7 lbs
Metric Height: 1.9 m
Metric Weight: 155.0 kg

Possible Moves: Agility, Bite, Burn Up, Crunch, Ember, Extreme Speed, Fire Fang, Flame Wheel, Flamethrower, Flare Blitz, Helping Hand, Howl, Leer, Play Rough

BASE STATS

			Min	Max
HP	78		266	360
Attack	84		155	293
Defense	78		144	280
Sp. Atk	109		200	348
Sp. Def	85		157	295
Speed	100		184	328
Total	534			

TYPE: STEEL

It has a body and heart of steel. Its glare is sufficient to make even an unruly Pokémon obey it.

How to Say It: Ko-ba-liyon
Imperial Height: 6' 11"
Imperial Weight: 551.2 lbs
Metric Height: 2.1 m
Metric Weight: 250 kg

Possible Moves: Confusion, Double Team, Lunar Dance, Moonlight, Psycho Cut, Psycho Shift, Safeguard, Mist

Kalos (Central)
Kanto

COBALION
Iron Will Pokemon

LEGENDARY POKEMON

BASE STATS

			Min	Max
HP	91		292	386
Attack	90		166	306
Defense	129		236	392
Sp. Atk	90		166	306
Sp. Def	72		134	267
Speed	108		198	346
Total	580			

COSMOEM
Protostar Pokémon

Kalos *(Central)*
Kanto

LEGENDARY POKEMON

TYPE: PSYCHIC

The king who ruled Alola in times of antiquity called it the "cocoon of the stars" and built an altar to worship it.

How to Say It: Cos-mo-em
Imperial Height: 0' 04"
Imperial Weight: 2204.4lbs
Metric Height: 0.1m
Metric Weight: 999.9kg

Possible Moves: Cosmic Power, Teleport

BASE STATS

Stat	Value		Min	Max
HP	43		196	290
Attack	29		56	172
Defense	131		240	397
Sp. Atk	29		56	172
Sp. Def	131		240	397
Speed	37		71	190
Total	400			

TYPE: Psychic

Even though its helpless, gaseous body can be blown away by the slightest breeze, it doesn't seem to care.

How to Say It: Cos-mog
Imperial Height: 0' 08"
Imperial Weight: 0.2lbs
Metric Height: 0.2m
Metric Weight: 0.1kg

Possible Moves: Splash, Teleport

Kalos *(Central)*
Kanto

COSMOG
Nebula Pokémon

LEGENDARY POKEMON

BASE STATS

				Min	Max
HP	43			196	290
Attack	29			56	172
Defense	31			60	177
Sp. Atk	29			56	172
Sp. Def	31			60	177
Speed	37			71	190
Total	200				

CRESSELIA
Lunar Pokemon

Kalos (Central)
Kanto

LEGENDARY POKEMON

TYPE: PSYCHIC

Shiny particles are released from its wings like a veil. It is said to represent the crescent moon.

How to Say It: Kri-se-la
Imperial Height: 4' 11"
Imperial Weight: 188.7 lbs
Metric Height: 1.5 m
Metric Weight: 85.6 kg

Possible Moves: Confusion, Double Team, Lunar Dance, Moonlight, Psycho Cut, Psycho Shift, Safeguard

BASE STATS

HP	120		350	444
Attack	70		130	262
Defense	120		220	372
Sp. Atk	75		139	273
Sp. Def	130		238	394
Speed	85		157	295
Total	600		Min	Max

TYPE: DARK

It chases people and Pokémon from its territory by causing them to experience deep, nightmarish slumbers.

How to Say It: DARK-rai
Imperial Height: 4' 11"
Imperial Weight: 111.3lbs
Metric Height: 1.5m
Metric Weight: 50.5kg

Possible Moves: Disable, Ominous Wind, Quick Attack, Hypnosis, Feint Attack, Nightmare, Double Team, Haze, Dark Void, Nasty Plot

Kalos *(Central)*
Kanto

DARKRAI
Pitch-Black Pokémon

MYTHICAL POKEMON

BASE STATS

			Min	Max
HP	70		250	344
Attack	90		166	306
Defense	90		166	306
Sp. Atk	135		247	405
Sp. Def	90		166	306
Speed	125		229	383
Total	600			

DEOXYS
(Attack Forme)
DNA Pokémon

Kalos (Central)
Kanto

MYTHICAL POKEMON

TYPE: PSYCHIC

The DNA of a space virus underwent a sudden mutation upon exposure to a laser beam and resulted in Deoxys. The crystalline organ on this Pokémon's chest appears to be its brain.

How to Say It: Deo-xys
Imperial Height: 5' 07"
Imperial Weight: 134.0lbs
Metric Height: 1.7m
Metric Weight: 60.8kg

Possible Moves: Leer, Wrap, Night Shade, Teleport, Knock Off, Pursuit, Psychic, Snatch, Psycho Shift, Zen Headbutt

BASE STATS

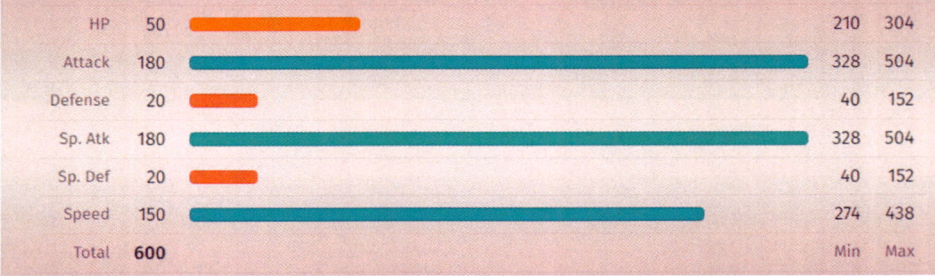

Stat	Base	Min	Max
HP	50	210	304
Attack	180	328	504
Defense	20	40	152
Sp. Atk	180	328	504
Sp. Def	20	40	152
Speed	150	274	438
Total	600		

TYPE: PSYCHIC

The DNA of a space virus underwent a sudden mutation upon exposure to a laser beam and resulted in Deoxys. The crystalline organ on this Pokémon's chest appears to be its brain.

How to Say It: Deo-xys
Imperial Height: 5' 07"
Imperial Weight: 134.0lbs
Metric Height: 1.7m
Metric Weight: 60.8kg

Possible Moves: Leer, Wrap, Night Shade, Teleport, Knock Off, Pursuit, Psychic, Snatch, Psycho Shift, Zen Headbutt, Cosmic Power, Recover

Kalos
(Central)
Kanto

DEOXYS
(Defense Form)

DNA Pokémon

MYHTHICAL POKEMON

BASE STATS

HP	50			210	304
Attack	70			130	262
Defense	160			292	460
Sp. Atk	70			130	262
Sp. Def	160			292	460
Speed	90			166	306
Total	600			Min	Max

TYPE: PSYCHIC

The DNA of a space virus underwent a sudden mutation upon exposure to a laser beam and resulted in Deoxys. The crystalline organ on this Pokémon's chest appears to be its brain.

How to Say It: Deo-xys
Imperial Height: 5' 07"
Imperial Weight: 134.0lbs
Metric Height: 1.7m
Metric Weight: 60.8kg

Possible Moves: Leer, Wrap, Night Shade, Teleport, Knock Off, Pursuit, Psychic, Snatch, Psycho Shift, Zen Headbutt, Cosmic Power, Recover

Kalos (Central)
Kanto

DEOXYS
(Normal Forme)
DNA Pokémon

MYTHICAL POKEMON

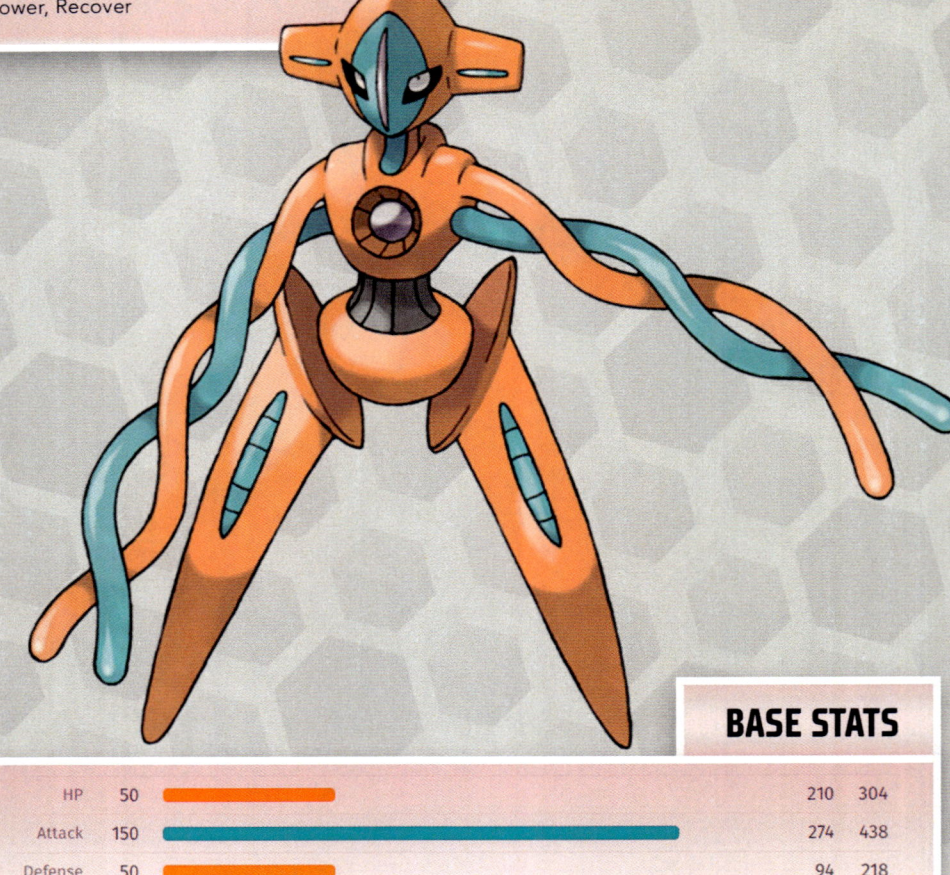

BASE STATS

			Min	Max
HP	50		210	304
Attack	150		274	438
Defense	50		94	218
Sp. Atk	150		274	438
Sp. Def	50		94	218
Speed	150		274	438
Total	600			

DEOXYS
(Speed Forme)

DNA Pokémon

Kalos (Central)
Kanto

MYTHICAL POKEMON

TYPE: PSYCHIC

The DNA of a space virus underwent a sudden mutation upon exposure to a laser beam and resulted in Deoxys. The crystalline organ on this Pokémon's chest appears to be its brain.

How to Say It: Deo-xys
Imperial Height: 5' 07"
Imperial Weight: 134.0lbs
Metric Height: 1.7m
Metric Weight: 60.8kg

Possible Moves: Leer, Wrap, Night Shade, Teleport, Knock Off, Pursuit, Psychic, Snatch, Psycho Shift, Zen Headbutt

BASE STATS

Stat	Value	Min	Max
HP	50	210	304
Attack	95	175	317
Defense	90	166	306
Sp. Atk	95	175	317
Sp. Def	90	166	306
Speed	180	328	504
Total	600		

DIALGA
Temporal Pokémon

Kalos
(Central)
Kanto

LEGENDARY POKEMON

TYPE: STEEL-DRAGON
A Pokémon spoken of in legend. It is said that time began moving when Dialga was born.

How to Say It: DI-al-ga
Imperial Height: 17' 09"
Imperial Weight: 1505.7lbs
Metric Height: 5.4m
Metric Weight: 683kg

Possible Moves: Dragon Breath, Scary Face, Metal Claw, Ancient Power, Slash, Power Gem, Metal Burst, Dragon Claw.

BASE STATS

			Min	Max
HP	100		310	404
Attack	120		220	372
Defense	120		220	372
Sp. Atk	150		274	438
Sp. Def	100		184	328
Speed	90		166	306
Total	680			

TYPE: ROCK-FAIRY

The impurities upon its body's surface have fallen away, and it sparkles so brilliantly when reflecting light that you cannot look directly at it. The diamond on its head measures over 2,000 carats.

How to Say It: Dian-so
Imperial Height: 2′ 04″
Imperial Weight: 19.4 lbs
Metric Height: 0.7 m
Metric Weight: 8.8 kg

Possible Moves: Harden, Rock Throw, Tackle, Sharpen, Smack Down, Reflect, Stealth Rock, Guard Split, Ancient Power, Flail, Skill Swap.

Kalos (Central)
Kanto

DIANCIE
[Mega Diancie]

Jewel Pokémon

MYTHICAL POKEMON

BASE STATS

Stat	Value		Min	Max
HP	50		210	304
Attack	100		184	328
Defense	150		274	438
Sp. Atk	100		184	328
Sp. Def	150		274	438
Speed	50		94	218
Total	600			

TYPE: ROCK-FAIRY

A sudden transformation of Carbink, its pink, glimmering body is said to be the loveliest sight in the whole world.

How to Say It: Dian-so
Imperial Height: 2' 04"
Imperial Weight: 19.4 lbs
Metric Height: 0.7 m
Metric Weight: 8.8 kg

Possible Moves: Harden, Rock Throw, Tackle, Sharpen, Smack Down, Reflect, Stealth Rock, Guard Split, Ancient Power, Flail, Skill Swap.

Kalos (Central)
Kanto

DIANCIE
Jewel Pokémon

MYTHICAL POKEMON

BASE STATS

		Min	Max
HP	50	210	304
Attack	100	184	328
Defense	150	274	438
Sp. Atk	100	184	328
Sp. Def	150	274	438
Speed	50	94	218
Total	600		

DRAGONITE
Dragon Pokémon

Kalos
(Central)
Kanto

TYPE: DRAGON-FLYING

It flies over raging seas as if they were nothing. Observing this, a ship's captain dubbed this Pokémon "the sea incarnate".

How to Say It: Dra-go-nait
Imperial Height: 7′ 03″
Imperial Weight: 463.0 lbs
Metric Height: 2.2 m
Metric Weight: 210.0 kg

Possible Moves: Aqua Jet, Dragon Rage, Fire Punch, Leer, Mist, Thunder Punch, Thunder Wave, Wing Attack, Wrap, Agility, Dragon Tail, Slam, Outrage

BASE STATS

HP	91		292	386
Attack	134		245	403
Defense	95		175	317
Sp. Atk	100		184	328
Sp. Def	100		184	328
Speed	80		148	284
Total	600		Min	Max

TYPE: NORMAL

The question of why only Eevee has such unstable genes has still not been solved.

How to Say It: Iv
Imperial Height: 1' 00"
Imperial Weight: 14.3 lbs
Metric Height: 0.3 m
Metric Weight: 6.5 kg

Possible Moves: Covet, Growl, Helping Hand, Tackle, Tail Whip, Sand Attack, Quick Attack, Baby-Doll Eyes, Swift Bite, Copycat, Baton Pass

Kalos *(Central)*
Kanto

EEVEE
Evolution Pokémon

BASE STATS

				Min	Max
HP	55			220	314
Attack	55			103	229
Defense	50			94	218
Sp. Atk	45			85	207
Sp. Def	65			121	251
Speed	55			103	229
Total	325				

ENTEI
Volcano Pokemon

Kalos (Central)
Kanto

LEGENDARY POKEMON

TYPE: FIRE

Entei embodies the passion of magma. This Pokémon is thought to have been born in the eruption of a volcano. It sends up massive bursts of fire that utterly consume all that they touch.

How to Say It: En-TE-I
Imperial Height: 6' 11"
Imperial Weight: 436.5 lbs
Metric Height: 2.1m
Metric Weight: 198 kg

Possible Moves: Bite, Eruption, Extrasensory, Lava Plume, Leer, Sacred Fire, Ember, Roar, Fire Spin, Stomp, Flamethrower, Swagger, Fire Fang

BASE STATS

			Min	Max
HP	115		340	434
Attack	115		211	361
Defense	85		157	295
Sp. Atk	90		166	306
Sp. Def	75		139	273
Speed	100		184	328
Total	580			

ETERNATUS

Gigantic Pokémon

LEGENDARY POKEMON

Kalos (Central)
Kanto

TYPE: POISON-DRAGON

The core on its chest absorbs energy emanating from the lands of the Galar region. This energy is what allows Eternatus to stay active.

How to Say It: E-ter-na-tus
Imperial Height: 65' 07"
Imperial Weight: 2094.4lbs
Metric Height: 20m
Metric Weight: 950kg

Possible Moves: Agility, Confuse Ray, Dragon Tail, Poison Tail, Toxic, Venoshock, Dragon Dance, Cross Poison, Dragon Pulse, Flamethrower.

BASE STATS

		Min	Max
HP	140	390	484
Attack	85	157	295
Defense	95	175	317
Sp. Atk	145	265	427
Sp. Def	95	175	317
Speed	130	238	394
Total	690		

TYPE: POISON- DRAGON

It was inside a meteorite that fell 20,000 years ago. There seems to be a connection between this Pokémon and the Dynamax phenomenon.

How to Say It: E-ter-na-max
Imperial Height: 328'01"
Imperial Weight: -
Metric Height: -
Metric Weight: 950kg

Possible Moves: Agility, Confuse Ray, Dragon Tail, Poison Tail, Toxic, Venoshock, Dragon Dance, Cross Poison, Dragon Pulse, Flamethrower

Kalos
(Central)
Kanto

ETERNATUS
(Eternamax)

Gigantic Pokémon

LEGENDARY POKEMON

BASE STATS

HP	255		620	714
Attack	115		211	361
Defense	250		454	658
Sp. Atk	125		229	383
Sp. Def	250		454	658
Speed	130		238	394
Total	1125		Min	Max

TYPE: GROUND-DRAGON

By flapping their wings, Flygon cause sandstorms that conceal Krookodile. The team then splits the prey they catch.

How to Say It: Flai-gon
Imperial Height: 6' 07"
Imperial Weight: 180.8 lbs
Metric Height: 2.0 m
Metric Weight: 82.0 kg

Possible Moves: Astonish, Bite, Bulldoze, Crunch, Dig, Dragon Breath, Dragon Claw, Dragon Dance, Feint, Fissure, Laser Focus, Sand Attack

Kalos
(Central)
Kanto

FLYGON
Mystic Pokémon

BASE STATS

HP	80		270	364
Attack	100		184	328
Defense	80		148	284
Sp. Atk	80		148	284
Sp. Def	80		148	284
Speed	100		184	328
Total	520		Min	Max

GARCHOMP
Dragon Pokémon

Kalos
(Central)
Kanto

TYPE: DRAGON-GROUND

It flies at the speed of sound while searching for prey, and it has midair battles with Salamence as the two compete for food.

How to Say It: Gar-champ
Imperial Height: 6' 03"
Imperial Weight: 209.4 lbs
Metric Height: 1.9 m
Metric Weight: 95.0 kg

Possible Moves: Crunch, Dragon Rage, Dual Chomp, Fire Fang, Sand Attack, Sandstorm, Tackle, Take Down, Sand Tomb, Slash, Dragon Claw

BASE STATS

			Min	Max
HP	108		326	420
Attack	130		238	394
Defense	95		175	317
Sp. Atk	80		148	284
Sp. Def	85		157	295
Speed	102		188	333
Total	600			

GARDEVOIR
Embrace Pokémon

Kalos (Central)
Kanto

TYPE: PSYCHIC-FAIRY

Gardevoir has the ability to read the future. If it senses impending danger to its Trainer, this Pokémon is said to unleash its psychokinetic energy at full power.

How to Say It: Gar-de-vor
Imperial Height: 5' 03"
Imperial Weight: 106.7 lbs
Metric Height: 1.6 m
Metric Weight: 48.4 kg

Possible Moves: Charm, Confusion, Dazzling Gleam, Disarming Voice, Double Team, Growl, Healing Wish, Misty Terrain, Moonblast, Hypnosis

BASE STATS

Stat	Value		Min	Max
HP	68		246	340
Attack	65		121	251
Defense	65		121	251
Sp. Atk	125		229	383
Sp. Def	115		211	361
Speed	80		148	284
Total	518			

GENESECT

Paleozoic Pokémon

Kalos (Central)
Kanto

MYTHICAL POKEMON

TYPE: BUG-STEEL

This ancient bug Pokémon was altered by Team Plasma. They upgraded the cannon on its back.

How to Say It: Ge-ne-sek
Imperial Height: 4' 11"
Imperial Weight: 181.9 lbs
Metric Height: 1.5 m
Metric Weight: 82.5 kg

Possible Moves: Fell Stinger, Magnet RIse, Metal Claw, Quick Attack, Screech, Techno Blast, Fury Cutter, Lock-on, Flame Charge, Magnet Bomb, Slash, Metal Sound

BASE STATS

			Min	Max
HP	71		252	346
Attack	120		220	372
Defense	95		175	317
Sp. Atk	120		220	372
Sp. Def	95		175	317
Speed	99		182	326
Total	600			

GENGAR
Shadow Pokémon

Kalos (Central)
Kanto

TYPE: GHOST-POISON

You can hear tales told all over the world about how Gengar will pay a visit to children who are naughty.

How to Say It: Bal-ba-sor
Imperial Height: 4' 11"
Imperial Weight: 89.9 lbs
Metric Height: 1.5 m
Metric Weight: 40.5 kg

Possible Moves: Confuse Ray, Hypnosis, Lick, Mean Look, Perish Song, Reflect Type, Shadow Punch, Payback, Spite, Curse, Hex, Night Shade, Sucker Punch, Dark Pulse

BASE STATS

Stat	Value		Min	Max
HP	60		230	324
Attack	65		121	251
Defense	60		112	240
Sp. Atk	130		238	394
Sp. Def	75		139	273
Speed	110		202	350
Total	500			

GIRATINA
(Origin Forme)

Renegade Pokémon

Kalos
(Central)

Kanto

LEGENDARY POKEMON

TYPE: GHOST-DRAGON

It was banished for its violence. It silently gazed upon the old world from the Distortion World.

How to Say It: GI-ra-TI-na
Imperial Height: 14' 09"
Imperial Weight: 1653.4lbs
Metric Height: 4.5m
Metric Weight: 750kg

Possible Moves: Dragon Breath, Scary Face, Ominous Wind, Ancient Power, Slash, Shadow Sneak, Destiny Bond, Dragon Claw, Earth Power.

BASE STATS

HP	150		410	504
Attack	100		184	328
Defense	120		220	372
Sp. Atk	100		184	328
Sp. Def	120		220	372
Speed	90		166	306
Total	680		Min	Max

GIRATINA
Renegade Pokémon

Kalos
(Central)
Kanto

LEGENDARY POKEMON

TYPE: GHOST-DRAGON

It was banished for its violence. It silently gazed upon the old world from the Distortion World.

How to Say It: GI-ra-TI-na
Imperial Height: 22′ 08″
Imperial Weight: 1433.0 lbs
Metric Height: 6.9 m
Metric Weight: 650 kg

Possible Moves: Dragon Breath, Scary Face, Ominous Wind, Ancient Power, Slash, Shadow Sneak, Destiny Bond, Dragon Claw, Earth Power.

BASE STATS

Stat	Value	Min	Max
HP	150	410	504
Attack	120	220	372
Defense	100	184	328
Sp. Atk	120	220	372
Sp. Def	100	184	328
Speed	90	166	306
Total	680		

GROUDON
(Primal Groudon)

Continent Pokémon

LEGENDARY POKEMON

Kalos
(Central)
Kanto

TYPE: GROUND-FIRE

Groudon is said to be the personification of the land itself. Legends tell of its many clashes against Kyogre, as each sought to gain the power of nature.

How to Say It: Gro-und
Imperial Height: 11' 06"
Imperial Weight: 2094.4lbs
Metric Height: 3.5m
Metric Weight: 950kg

Possible Moves: Ancient Power, Mud Shot, Scary Face, Earth Power, Lava Plume, Rest, Earthquake, Precipice Blade.

BASE STATS

		Min	Max
HP	100	310	404
Attack	180	328	504
Defense	160	292	460
Sp. Atk	150	274	438
Sp. Def	90	166	306
Speed	90	166	306
Total	770		

GROUDON

Continent Pokémon

Kalos *(Central)*
Kanto

LEGENDARY POKEMON

TYPE: GROUND

Groudon is said to be the personification of the land itself. Legends tell of its many clashes against Kyogre, as each sought to gain the power of nature.

How to Say It: Gro-und
Imperial Height: 11' 06"
Imperial Weight: 2094.4lbs
Metric Height: 3.5m
Metric Weight: 950kg

Possible Moves: Ancient Power, Mud Shot, Scary Face, Earth Power, Lava Plume, Rest, Earthquake, Precipice Blade.

BASE STATS

Stat	Value		Min	Max
HP	100		310	404
Attack	150		274	438
Defense	140		256	416
Sp. Atk	100		184	328
Sp. Def	90		166	306
Speed	90		166	306
Total	670			

GUZZLORD

EON Pokemon

LEGENDARY POKEMON

Kalos (Central)
Kanto

TYPE: DARK-DRAGON

Although it's alien to this world and a danger here, it's apparently a common organism in the world where it normally lives.

How to Say It: Gaz-lord
Imperial Height: 18' 01"
Imperial Weight: 1957.7 lbs
Metric Height: 5.5 m
Metric Weight: 888 kg

Possible Moves: Belch, Bite, Dragon Rage, Stockpile, Swallow, Wide Guard, Stomp, Brutal Swing, Steamroller, Dragon Tail, Iron Tail, Stomping Tantrium

BASE STATS

HP	223		556	650
Attack	101		186	331
Defense	53		99	225
Sp. Atk	97		179	322
Sp. Def	53		99	225
Speed	43		81	203
Total	570		Min	Max

HEATRAN

Lava Dome Pokemon

Kalos
(Central)
Kanto

LEGENDARY POKEMON

TYPE: FIRE-STEEL

It dwells in volcanic caves. It digs in with its cross-shaped feet to crawl on ceilings and walls.

How to Say It: HIT-ran
Imperial Height: 5' 07"
Imperial Weight: 948.0 lbs
Metric Height: 1.7m
Metric Weight: 430 kg

Possible Moves: Ancient Power, Earth Power, Fire Spin, Heat Wave, Iron Head, Magma Storm, Leer, Fire Fang, Metal Sound

BASE STATS

Stat	Value	Min	Max
HP	91	292	386
Attack	90	166	306
Defense	106	195	342
Sp. Atk	130	238	394
Sp. Def	106	195	342
Speed	77	143	278
Total	600		

Ho-Oh

Rainbow Pokémon

Kalos (Central)
Kanto

LEGENDARY POKEMON

TYPE: FIRE/FLYING

Ho-Oh's feathers glow in seven colors depending on the angle at which they are struck by light. These feathers are said to bring happiness to the bearers. This Pokémon is said to live at the foot of a rainbow.

How to Say It: Ho-OH
Imperial Height: 12'06"
Imperial Weight: 438.7lbs
Metric Height: 3.8m
Metric Weight: 199kg

Possible Moves: Winter Ball, Whirlwind, Gust, Brave Bird, Extrasensory, Sunny Day, Fire Blast, Sacred Fire, Punishment.

BASE STATS

Stat	Value		Min	Max
HP	106		322	416
Attack	130		238	394
Defense	90		166	306
Sp. Atk	110		202	350
Sp. Def	154		281	447
Speed	90		166	306
Total	680		Min	Max

HOOPA
(Hoopa Confined)

Mischief Pokémon

Kalos
(Central)
Kanto

MYTHICAL POKEMON

TYPE: PSYCHIC-GHOST

In its true form, it possess a huge amount of power. Legends of its avarice tell how it once carried off an entire castle to gain the treasure hidden within.

How to Say It: Hoo-pa
Imperial Height: 1' 08"
Imperial Weight: 19.8lbs
Metric Height: 0.5m
Metric Weight: 9kg

Possible Moves: Ally Switch, Confusion, Destiny Bond, Hyperspace Hole, Trick, Astonish, Magic Coat, Light Screen

BASE STATS

Stat	Value		Min	Max
HP	80		270	364
Attack	110		202	350
Defense	60		112	240
Sp. Atk	150		274	438
Sp. Def	130		238	394
Speed	70		130	262
Total	600			

TYPE: PSYCHIC-GHOST

In its true form, it possess a huge amount of power. Legends of its avarice tell how it once carried off an entire castle to gain the treasure hidden within.

How to Say It: Hoo-pa
Imperial Height: 2' 04"
Imperial Weight: 20.9 lbs
Metric Height: 0.7m
Metric Weight: 9.5kg

Possible Moves: Ally Switch, Confusion, Destiny Bond, Hyperspace Hole, Trick, Astonish, Magic Coat, Light Screen, Pysbeam, Skill Swap

Kalos (Central)
Kanto

HOOPA
(Hoopa Unbound)

Djinn Pokémonn

MYTHICAL POKEMON

BASE STATS

HP	80		270	364
Attack	160		292	460
Defense	60		112	240
Sp. Atk	170		310	482
Sp. Def	130		238	394
Speed	80		148	284
Total	680		Min	Max

TYPE: FIRE-FIGHTING

Its crown of fire is indicative of its fiery nature. It is beaten by none in terms of quickness.

Kalos (Central)
Kanto

INFERNAPE
Gleam Eyes Pokémon

How to Say It: In-fer-ape
Imperial Height: 3' 11"
Imperial Weight: 121.3 lbs
Metric Height: 1.2 m
Metric Weight: 55.0 kg

Possible Moves: Close Combat, Ember, Flare Blitz, Leer, Mach Punch, Scratch, Taunt, Fury Swipes, Flame Wheel, Feint

BASE STATS

			Min	Max
HP	76		262	356
Attack	104		191	337
Defense	71		132	265
Sp. Atk	104		191	337
Sp. Def	71		132	265
Speed	108		198	346
Total	534			

JIRACHI

Wish Pokémon

Kalos (Central)
Kanto

MYTHICAL POKEMON

TYPE: STEEL-PSYCHIC

A legend states that Jirachi will make true any wish that is written on notes attached to its head when it awakens. If this Pokémon senses danger, it will fight without awakening.

How to Say It: Ji-ra-chi
Imperial Height: 1' 00"
Imperial Weight: 2.4lbs
Metric Height: 0.3m
Metric Weight: 1.1kg

Possible Moves: Confusion, Wish, Swift, Helping Hand, Life Dew, Zen Headbutt, Gravity, Psychic, Meteor Mash

BASE STATS

Stat	Value		Min	Max
HP	100		310	404
Attack	100		184	328
Defense	100		184	328
Sp. Atk	100		184	328
Sp. Def	100		184	328
Speed	100		184	328
Total	600			

KARTANA
Drawn Sword Pokémon

LEGENDARY POKEMON

TYPE: GRASS-STEEL

This Ultra Beast's body, which is as thin as paper, is like a sharpened sword.

Kalos *(Central)*
Kanto

How to Say It: Kar-Ta-na
Imperial Height: 1' 00"
Imperial Weight: 0.2 lbs
Metric Height: 0.3 m
Metric Weight: 0.1 kg

Possible Moves: Charge, Spark, Tail Glow, Thunder Shock, Wrap, Thunder Wave, Shock Wave, Ingrain, Thunder Punch, Eerie Impulse, Signal Beam

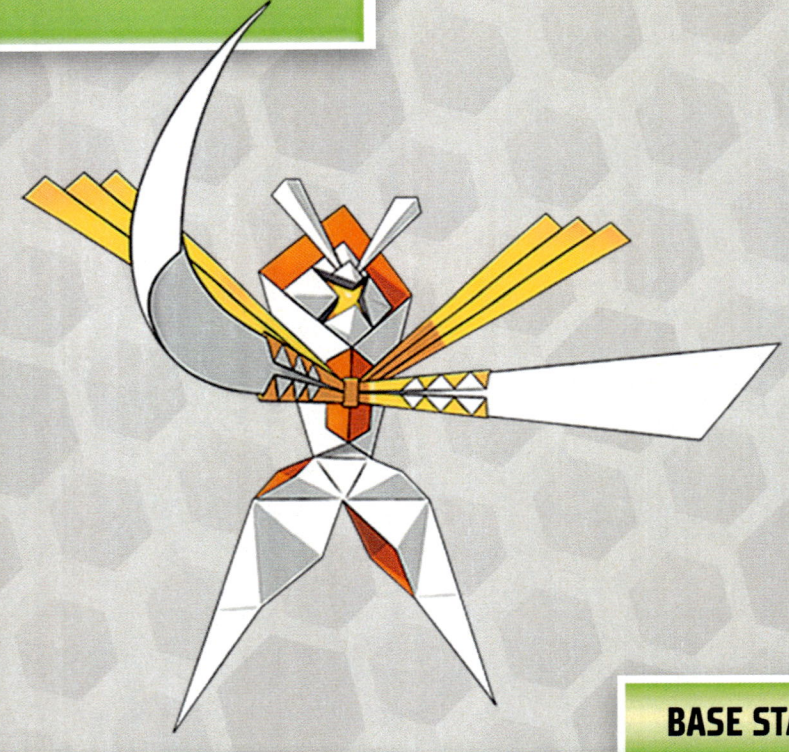

BASE STATS

Stat	Value		Min	Max
HP	59		228	322
Attack	181		330	507
Defense	131		240	397
Sp. Atk	59		110	238
Sp. Def	31		60	177
Speed	109		200	348
Total	570		Min	Max

KELDEO
[Resolute Form]

Colt Pokémon

MYTHICAL POKEMON

Kalos (Central)
Kanto

TYPE: WATER-FIGHTING

It crosses the world, running over the surfaces of oceans and rivers. It appears at scenic waterfronts.

How to Say It: Kel-deo
Imperial Height: 4' 07"
Imperial Weight: 106.9lbs
Metric Height: 1.4m
Metric Weight: 48.5kg

Possible Moves: Aqua Jet, Helping Hand, Leer, Secret Sword, Work Up, Bubble Beam, Quick Guard, Double Kick, Retaliate, Aqua Tail, Take Down

BASE STATS

			Min	Max
HP	91		292	386
Attack	72		134	267
Defense	90		166	306
Sp. Atk	129		236	392
Sp. Def	90		166	306
Speed	108		198	346
Total	580			

KELDEO

Colt Pokémon

Kalos (Central)
Kanto

MYTHICAL POKEMON

TYPE: WATER-FIGHTING

It crosses the world, running over the surfaces of oceans and rivers. It appears at scenic waterfronts.

How to Say It: Kel-deo
Imperial Height: 4' 07"
Imperial Weight: 106.9 lbs
Metric Height: 1.4 m
Metric Weight: 48.5 kg

Possible Moves: Aqua Jet, Helping Hand, Leer, Secret Sword, Work Up, Bubble Beam, Quick Guard, Double Kick, Retaliate, Aqua Tail, Take Down, Sacred Sword, Swords Dance

BASE STATS

HP	91	292	386
Attack	72	134	267
Defense	90	166	306
Sp. Atk	129	236	392
Sp. Def	90	166	306
Speed	108	198	346
Total	580	Min	Max

TYPE: FIGHTING

It evolves into Urshifu when shown the scroll in one of the Towers of Two Fists. The form it evolves into depends on the tower it is trained in.

How to Say It: Kub-fu
Imperial Height: 2′ 00″
Imperial Weight: 26.5 lbs
Metric Height: 0.6 m
Metric Weight: 12.0 kg

Possible Moves: Leer, Rock Smash, Endure, Focus Energy, Aerial Ace, Scary Face, Headbutt, Brick Break, Detect, Bulk Up, Iron Head, Dynamic Punch, Counter

Kalos
(Central)
Kanto

KUBFU
Wushu Pokémon

LEGENDARY POKEMON

BASE STATS

			Min	Max
HP	60		230	324
Attack	90		166	306
Defense	60		112	240
Sp. Atk	53		99	225
Sp. Def	50		94	218
Speed	72		134	267
Total	385			

TYPE: WATER

It is said to have widened the seas by causing downpours. It had been asleep in a marine trench.

How to Say It: Kyo-gre
Imperial Height: 32' 02"
Imperial Weight: 948.0 lbs
Metric Height: 9.8 m
Metric Weight: 430.0 kg

Possible Moves: Ancient Power, Water Pulse, Scary Face, Aqua Tail, Body Slam, Aqua Ring, Ice Beam, Origin Pulse, Calm Mind, Muddy Water, Sheer Cold.

Kalos *(Central)*
Kanto

KYOGRE
[Primal Kyogre]

Sea Basin Pokémon

LEGENDARY POKEMON

BASE STATS

Stat	Value		Min	Max
HP	100		310	404
Attack	150		274	438
Defense	90		166	306
Sp. Atk	180		328	504
Sp. Def	160		292	460
Speed	90		166	306
Total	770		Min	Max

TYPE: WATER

Through Primal Reversion and with nature's full power, it will take back its true form. It can summon storms that cause the sea levels to rise.

How to Say It: Kyo-gre
Imperial Height: 14' 09"
Imperial Weight: 776.0lbs
Metric Height: 4.5m
Metric Weight: 352kg

Possible Moves: Ancient Power, Water Pulse, Scary Face, Aqua Tail, Body Slam, Aqua Ring, Ice Beam, Origin Pulse, Calm Mind, Muddy Water, Sheer Cold.

Kalos
(Central)
Kanto

KYOGRE
Sea Basin Pokémon

LEGENDARY POKEMON

BASE STATS

Stat	Value		Min	Max
HP	100		310	404
Attack	100		184	328
Defense	90		166	306
Sp. Atk	150		274	438
Sp. Def	140		256	416
Speed	90		166	306
Total	670			

TYPE: DRAGON-ICE

It generates a powerful, freezing energy inside itself, but its body became frozen when the energy leaked out.

How to Say It: Kyu-rem
Imperial Height: 10' 10"
Imperial Weight: 716.5 lbs
Metric Height: 3.3 m
Metric Weight: 325.0 kg

Possible Moves: Ancient Power, Dragon Breath, Freezy-dry, Noble Roar, Slash, Endeavor, Dragon Pulse, Ice Beam, Hyper Voice.

Kalos
(Central)
Kanto

KYUREM
(Black Kyurem)

Boundary Pokémon

LEGENDARY POKEMON

BASE STATS

			Min	Max
HP	125		360	454
Attack	170		310	482
Defense	100		184	328
Sp. Atk	120		220	372
Sp. Def	90		166	306
Speed	95		175	317
Total	700			

TYPE: DRAGON-ICE

The sameness of Reshiram's and Kyurem's genes allowed Kyurem to absorb Reshiram. Kyurem can now use the power of both fire and ice.

How to Say It: Kyu-rem
Imperial Height: 11' 10"
Imperial Weight: 716.5lbs
Metric Height: 3.6 m
Metric Weight: 325.0 kg

Possible Moves: Ancient Power, Dragon Breath, Freezy-dry, Noble Roar, Slash, Endeavor, Dragon Pulse, Ice Beam, Hyper Voice.

Kalos (Central)
Kanto

KYUREM
(White Kyurem)

Boundary Pokémon

LEGENDARY POKEMON

BASE STATS

			Min	Max
HP	125		360	454
Attack	120		220	372
Defense	90		166	306
Sp. Atk	170		310	482
Sp. Def	100		184	328
Speed	95		175	317
Total	700			

TYPE: DRAGON-ICE

This legendary ice Pokémon waits for a hero to fill in the missing parts of its body with truth or ideals.

How to Say It: Kyu-rem
Imperial Height: 9' 10"
Imperial Weight: 716.5lbs
Metric Height: 3m
Metric Weight: 325kg

Possible Moves: Ancient Power, Dragon Breath, Freezy-dry, Noble Roar, Slash, Endeavor, Dragon Pulse, Ice Beam, Hyper Voice.

Kalos *(Central)*
Kanto

KYUREM
Boundary Pokémon

LEGENDARY POKEMON

BASE STATS

			Min	Max
HP	125		360	454
Attack	130		238	394
Defense	90		166	306
Sp. Atk	130		238	394
Sp. Def	90		166	306
Speed	95		175	317
Total	660			

LANDORUS
(Therian Forme)

Abundance Pokémon

Kalos *(Central)*
Kanto

LEGENDARY POKEMON

TYPE: GROUND-FLYING

The energy that comes pouring from its tail increases the nutrition in the soil, making crops grow to great size.

How to Say It: Lan-do-rus
Imperial Height: 4' 03"
Imperial Weight: 149.9 lbs
Metric Height: 1.3 m
Metric Weight: 68.0 kg

Possible Moves: Block, Fissure, Hammer Arm, Imprison, Mud Shot, Outrage, Rock Tomb, Punishment, Bulldoze, Rock Throw

BASE STATS

			Min	Max
HP	89		288	382
Attack	145		265	427
Defense	90		166	306
Sp. Atk	105		193	339
Sp. Def	80		148	284
Speed	91		168	309
Total	600			

LANDORUS
(Incarnate Forme)

Abundance Pokémon

LEGENDARY POKEMON

Kalos *(Central)*
Kanto

TYPE: GROUND-FLYING

Lands visited by Landorus grant such bountiful crops that it has been hailed as "The Guardian of the Fields."

How to Say It: Lan-do-rus
Imperial Height: 4' 11"
Imperial Weight: 149.9 lbs
Metric Height: 1.5m
Metric Weight: 68 kg

Possible Moves: Block, Fissure, Hammer Arm, Imprison, Mud Shot, Outrage, Rock Tomb, Punishment, Bulldoze, Rock Throw

BASE STATS

HP	89		288	382
Attack	125		229	383
Defense	90		166	306
Sp. Atk	115		211	361
Sp. Def	80		148	284
Speed	101		186	331
Total	600		Min	Max

LATIAS
[Mega Latias]

EON Pokemon

LEGENDARY POKEMON

Kalos
(Central)
Kanto

TYPE: DRAGON-PSYCHIC

Its body is covered with a down that can refract light in such a way that it becomes invisible.

How to Say It: LA-Ti-As
Imperial Height: 5' 11"
Imperial Weight: 114.6 lbs
Metric Height: 1.8 m
Metric Weight: 52 kg

Possible Moves: Healing Wish, Helping Hand, Psywave, Safeguard, Wish, Water Sport, Charm, Stored Power

BASE STATS

Stat	Value		Min	Max
HP	80		270	364
Attack	100		184	328
Defense	120		220	372
Sp. Atk	140		256	416
Sp. Def	150		274	438
Speed	110		202	350
Total	700			

LATIAS

EON Pokemon

Kalos (Central)
Kanto

LEGENDARY POKEMON

TYPE: DRAGON-PSYCHIC

Latias is highly sensitive to the emotions of people. If it senses any hostility, this Pokémon ruffles the feathers all over its body and cries shrilly to intimidate the foe.

How to Say It: LA-Ti-As
Imperial Height: 4' 07"
Imperial Weight: 88.2 lbs
Metric Height: 1.4 m
Metric Weight: 40 kg

Possible Moves: Healing Wish, Helping Hand, Psywave, Safeguard, Wish, Water Sport, Charm, Stored Power

BASE STATS

Stat	Value	Min	Max
HP	80	270	364
Attack	80	148	284
Defense	90	166	306
Sp. Atk	110	202	350
Sp. Def	130	238	394
Speed	110	202	350
Total	600		

TYPE: DRAGON-PSYCHIC

It has a docile temperament and dislikes fighting. Tucking in its forelegs, it can fly faster than a jet plane.

How to Say It: La-Tios
Imperial Height: 7' 07"
Imperial Weight: 154.3 lbs
Metric Height: 2.3 m
Metric Weight: 70 kg

Possible Moves: Heal Block, Helping Hand, Memento, Psywave, Safeguard, Protect, Dragon Dance, Stored Power

Kalos
(Central)
Kanto

LATIOS
[Mega Latios]

Eon Pokémon

LEGENDARY POKEMON

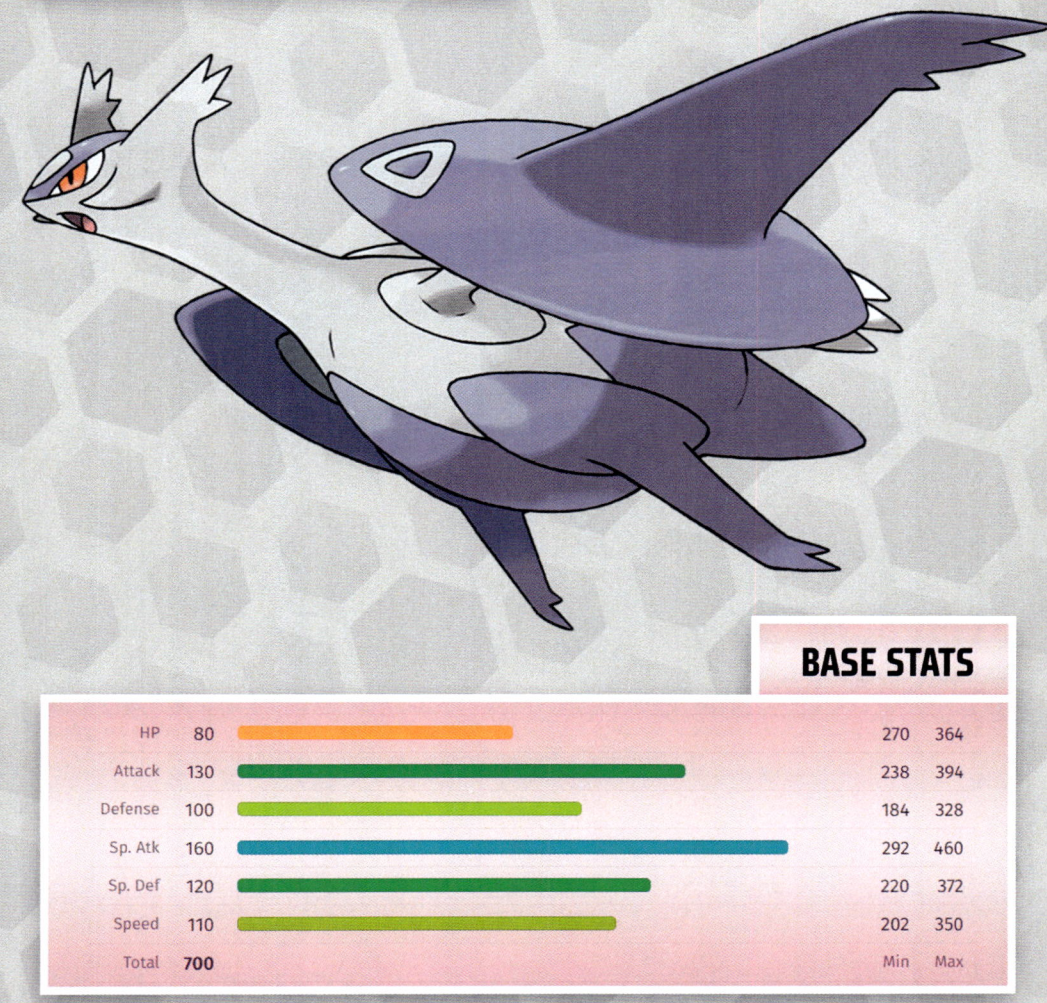

BASE STATS

			Min	Max
HP	80		270	364
Attack	130		238	394
Defense	100		184	328
Sp. Atk	160		292	460
Sp. Def	120		220	372
Speed	110		202	350
Total	700			

TYPE: DRAGON-PSYCHIC

Latios has the ability to make others see an image of what it has seen or imagines in its head. This Pokémon is intelligent and understands human speech.

How to Say It: La-Tios
Imperial Height: 6' 07"
Imperial Weight: 132.3 lbs
Metric Height: 2 m
Metric Weight: 60 kg

Possible Moves: Heal Block, Helping Hand, Memento, Psywave, Safeguard, Protect, Dragon Dance, Stored Power

Kalos
(Central)
Kanto

LATIOS
Eon Pokémon

LEGENDARY POKEMON

BASE STATS

Stat	Value		Min	Max
HP	80		270	364
Attack	90		166	306
Defense	80		148	284
Sp. Atk	130		238	394
Sp. Def	110		202	350
Speed	110		202	350
Total	600		Min	Max

TYPE: FIGHTING-STEEL

It concentrates its mental energy and fires off mysterious waves called auras, which can crush boulders of large size to dust.

How to Say It: Lu-ka-rio
Imperial Height: 3' 11"
Imperial Weight: 54.0 lbs
Metric Height: 1.2 m
Metric Weight: 54.0 kg

Possible Moves: Aura Sphere, Copycat, Detect, Feint, Final Gambit, Force Palm, Helping Hand, Life Dew, Metal Claw, Nasty Plot, Quick Attack, Reversal, Rock Smash,

Kalos (Central)
Kanto

LUCARIO
Aura Pokémon

BASE STATS

			Min	Max
HP	70		250	344
Attack	110		202	350
Defense	70		130	262
Sp. Atk	115		211	361
Sp. Def	70		130	262
Speed	90		166	306
Total	525			

TYPE: PSYCHIC-FLYING

Lugia's wings pack devastating power—a light fluttering of its wings can blow apart regular houses. As a result, this Pokémon chooses to live out of sight deep under the sea.

How to Say It: Lu-gia
Imperial Height: 17' 01"
Imperial Weight: 476.2lbs
Metric Height: 5.2m
Metric Weight: 216kg

Possible Moves: Weather Ball, Whirlwind, Gust, Dragon Rush, Extrasensory, Rain Dance, Hydro Pump, Aeroblast, Punishment, Ancient Power.

Kalos
(Central)
Kanto

LUGIA
Diving Pokémon

LEGENDARY POKEMON

BASE STATS

				Min	Max
HP	106			322	416
Attack	90			166	306
Defense	130			238	394
Sp. Atk	90			166	306
Sp. Def	154			281	447
Speed	110			202	350
Total	680				

Lunala
Moone Pokémon

Kalos (Central)
Kanto

LEGENDARY POKEMON

TYPE: PSYCHIC-GHOST

Records of it exist in writings from long, long ago, where it was known by the name "the beast that calls the moon".

How to Say It: Lu-na-la
Imperial Height: 13' 01"
Imperial Weight: 264.6lbs
Metric Height: 4m
Metric Weight: 120kg

Possible Moves: Confusion. Cosmic Power, Hypnosis, Moongeist Beam, Teleport, Night Shade, Confuse Ray, Air Slash, Shadow Ball, Moonlight, Night Daze

BASE STATS

HP	137	384	478
Attack	113	207	357
Defense	89	164	304
Sp. Atk	137	251	410
Sp. Def	107	197	344
Speed	97	179	322
Total	680	Min	Max

LUXRAY

Gleam Eyes Pokémon

TYPE: WATER

When its eyes gleam gold, it can spot hiding prey—even those taking shelter behind a wall.

Kalos *(Central)*
Kanto

How to Say It: Lask-ray
Imperial Height: 4' 07"
Imperial Weight: 92.6 lbs
Metric Height: 1.4 m
Metric Weight: 42.0 kg

Possible Moves: Flash Cannon, Tackle, Tail Whip, Water Gun, Withdraw, Rapid Spin, Bite, Water Pulse, Protect, Rain Dance

BASE STATS

Stat	Value		Min	Max
HP	80		270	364
Attack	120		220	372
Defense	79		146	282
Sp. Atk	95		175	317
Sp. Def	79		146	282
Speed	70		130	262
Total	523			

MAGEARNA

Artificial Pokémon

Kalos (Central)
Kanto

MYTHICAL POKEMON

TYPE: STEEL-FAIRY

It synchronizes its consciousness with others to understand their feelings. This faculty makes it useful for taking care of people.

How to Say It: Ma-gir-na
Imperial Height: 3' 03"
Imperial Weight: 177.5 lbs
Metric Height: 1 m
Metric Weight: 80.5 kg

Possible Moves: Crafty Shield, Defense Curl, Gear Up, Helping Hand, Iron Head, Psybeam, Shift Gear, Sonic Boom, Lucky Chant, Aurora Beam, Mirror Shot, Mind Reader, Flash Cannon

BASE STATS

HP	80		270	364
Attack	95		175	317
Defense	115		211	361
Sp. Atk	130		238	394
Sp. Def	115		211	361
Speed	65		121	251
Total	600		Min	Max

MANAPHY
Seafaring Pokémon

Kalos
(Central)
Kanto

MYTHICAL POKEMON

TYPE: WATER

It is born with a wondrous power that lets it bond with any kind of Pokémon.

How to Say It: Ma-na-phy
Imperial Height: 1' 00"
Imperial Weight: 3.1lbs
Metric Height: 0.3m
Metric Weight: 1.4kg

Possible Moves: Bubble, Tail Glow, Water Sport, Charm, Supersonic, Bubble Beam, Acid Armor, Whirlpool, Water Pulse, Aqua Ring

BASE STATS

Stat	Value		Min	Max
HP	100		310	404
Attack	100		184	328
Defense	100		184	328
Sp. Atk	100		184	328
Sp. Def	100		184	328
Speed	100		184	328
Total	600			

TYPE: FIGHTING-GHOST

It slips into the shadows of others and mimics their powers and movements. As it improves, it becomes stronger than those it's imitating.

How to Say It: Mar-sha-dou
Imperial Height: 2' 04"
Imperial Weight: 48.9 lbs
Metric Height: 0.7 m
Metric Weight: 22.2 kg

Possible Moves: Copycat, Counter Feint, Fire Punch, Ice Punch, Shadow Sneak, Thunder Punch, Role Play,

Kalos (Central)
Kanto

MARSHADOW

Gloomdweller Pokémon

MYTHICAL POKEMON

BASE STATS

			Min	Max
HP	90		290	384
Attack	125		229	383
Defense	80		148	284
Sp. Atk	90		166	306
Sp. Def	90		166	306
Speed	125		229	383
Total	600			

MELMETAL
Hex Nut Pokémon

Kalos *(Central)*
Kanto

MYTHICAL POKEMON

TYPE: STEEL

Revered long ago for its capacity to create iron from nothing, for some reason it has come back to life after 3,000 years.

How to Say It: Ge-ne-sek
Imperial Height: 8' 02"
Imperial Weight: 1763.7 lbs
Metric Height: 2.5 m
Metric Weight: 800.0 kg

Possible Moves: Harden, Headbutt, Tail Whip, Thunder Punch, Thunder Shock, Thunder Wave, Acid Armor, Flash Cannon, Mega Punch, Protect, Discharge, Dynamic Punch

BASE STATS

HP	135		380	474
Attack	143		261	423
Defense	143		261	423
Sp. Atk	80		148	284
Sp. Def	65		121	251
Speed	34		65	183
Total	600		Min	Max

TYPE: NORMAL-PSYCHIC

The melodies sung by Meloetta have the power to make Pokémon that hear them happy or sad.

How to Say It: Me-lo-ita
Imperial Height: 2' 00"
Imperial Weight: 14.3 lbs
Metric Height: 0.6 m
Metric Weight: 6.5 kg

Possible Moves: Confusion, Quick Attack, Round, Sing, Teeter Dance, Acrobatics, Psybeam, Echoed Voice, U-turn, Wake-Up Slap, Psychic, Hyper Voice

Kalos (Central)
Kanto

MELOETTA
[Aria Forme]

Melody Pokémon

MYTHICAL POKEMON

BASE STATS

HP	100		310	404
Attack	77		143	278
Defense	77		143	278
Sp. Atk	128		234	390
Sp. Def	128		234	390
Speed	90		166	306
Total	600		Min	Max

TYPE: NORMAL-FIGHTING

The melodies sung by Meloetta have the power to make Pokémon that hear them happy or sad.

How to Say It: Me-lo-ita
Imperial Height: 2' 00"
Imperial Weight: 14.3 lbs
Metric Height: 0.6 m
Metric Weight: 6.5 kg

Possible Moves: Confusion, Quick Attack, Round, Sing, Teeter Dance, Acrobatics, Psybeam, Echoed Voice, U-turn, Wake-Up Slap, Psychic, Hyper Voice

Kalos (Central)
Kanto

MELOETTA
(Piroutte Forme)

Melody Pokémon

MYTHICAL POKEMON

BASE STATS

				Min	Max
HP	100			310	404
Attack	128			234	390
Defense	90			166	306
Sp. Atk	77			143	278
Sp. Def	77			143	278
Speed	128			234	390
Total	600				

TYPE: STEEL

It melts particles of iron and other metals found in the subsoil, so it can absorb them into its body of molten steel.

How to Say It: Mel-tan
Imperial Height: 0′ 08″
Imperial Weight: 17.6 lbs
Metric Height: 0.2 m
Metric Weight: 8.0 kg

Possible Moves: Harden, Thunder Shock, Tail Whip, Headbutt, Acid Armor, Flash Cannon

Kalos (Central)
Kanto

MELTAN
Hex Nut Pokémon

MYTHICAL POKEMON

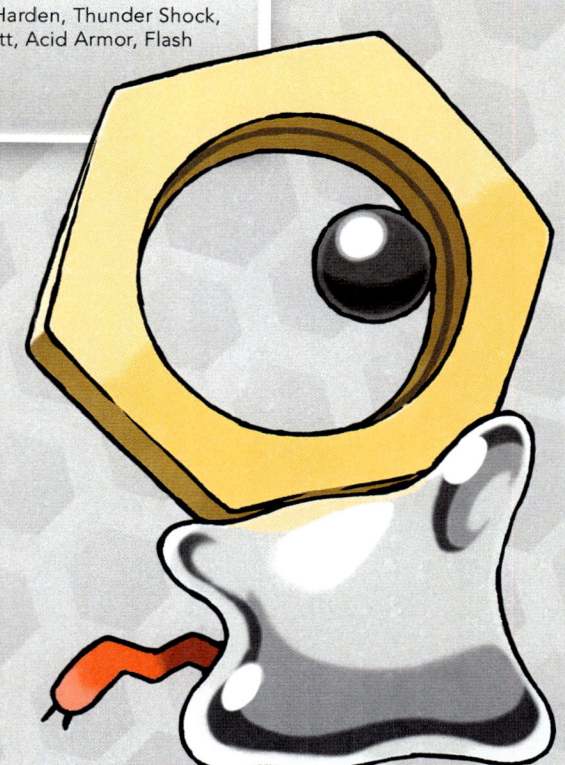

BASE STATS

			Min	Max
HP	46		202	296
Attack	65		121	251
Defense	65		121	251
Sp. Atk	55		103	229
Sp. Def	35		67	185
Speed	34		65	183
Total	300			

Made in the USA
Monee, IL
20 December 2020